CAMPING
and
ORIENTEERING

Michael Jay

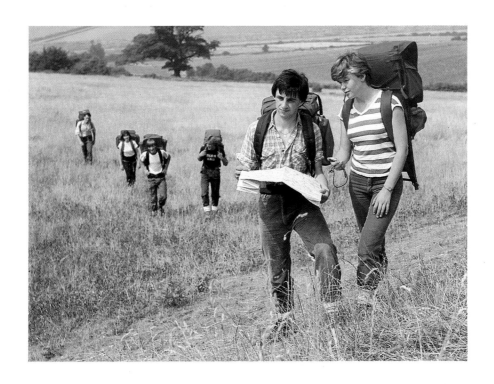

Warwick Press

Designed and produced by:
David Jefferis

Edited by:
Jackie Gaff

Illustrated by:
Rhoda and Robert Burns
James Robins
Michael Roffe

Library of Congress Cataloging-in-Publication Data

Jay, Michael.
   Camping and orienteering / Michael Jay.
     p. cm. – (Adventure sports)
     Summary: A guide to planning and enjoying a camping trip, with
tips on reading maps, preparing for adverse weather conditions,
building a fire, and including an introduction to competitive
orienteering.
    ISBN 0-531-19083-8
    1. Camping – Juvenile literature. 2. Orientation – Juvenile
literature. [1. Camping.] I. Title. II. Series.
GV191.7.J39 1990
796.54–dc20   8977474
                                   CIP
                                   AC

Published in 1990 by Warwick Press,
387 Park Avenue South, New York, New York 10016.

First published in 1990 by Kingfisher Books Ltd.

Printed in Spain

Contents

The great outdoors

■ There are few better ways to discover the world of nature than by taking a camping trip. As well as the daytime adventures of exploring the countryside, there's the excitement of sleeping under canvas or even the stars. Never camp alone, though. Besides being safer if you have an accident or get lost, sharing your trip with friends will add to your fun.

Your trip will also be safer and more enjoyable if you take time to prepare for it carefully, choosing the correct equipment and improving your map-reading and survival skills.

▶ Most people's idea of a perfect camping trip includes beautiful weather and spectacular scenery. It's always wise to be prepared for the worst as well as the best, though. Armed with the correct equipment, you'll have a good time whether it rains or shines.

▶ There are lots of different ways to go camping. Although you'll cover more distance on wheels than on foot, without a special mountain bike you'll be limited to paved roads.

If you're planning to keep on the move, make sure you travel light. A way of avoiding the weight problem is to choose one site as a base camp for day trips. This is called a "standing camp."

Night life

Curled up in bed at home, you may not have realized that there's a whole world of animals which become active when the Sun goes down. On a camping trip you'll hear the owls hooting and the faint high-pitched squeaks that bats make as they fly about at sunset. Little scurrying noises come from mice and other small rodents, busy searching for food. If you're lucky — and very quiet — you may even see larger animals of the night, such as foxes and opossums.

Prepare for adventure!

■ Good equipment is essential for any camping trip, and lightweight items will take the hard work out of walking with a pack on your back. Make sure you don't carry things you won't really need on the trip.

Most large towns have specialist camping stores — call and ask about catalogs if you live too far away to visit. Enquire about renting equipment if you don't want to buy the bigger items, such as tents or sleeping bags.

Pack clothes for rain and sun, cold, and heat. A short rainproof and windproof jacket with a hood is essential. Wear layers of clothes against the cold, such as long johns or tights under your jeans.

Footwear is very important, and you should always wear in new shoes or boots before you set off. Take proper hiking boots, or sturdy shoes with contoured soles — smooth soles are slippery on wet ground. If you plan to walk far, put on an extra pair of thick socks to protect your feet from blistering.

Pack a sunhat for hot weather, and a good sunscreening lotion to protect vulnerable spots such as your nose and the back of your neck.

Simple quilting

Wall quilting

▲ You need to keep warm to sleep properly. A sleeping mat will protect you from the cold ground, as well as cushioning you from bumps and stones. Camping stores sell special mats, but layers of newspaper can do the job more cheaply.

Take a good sleeping bag. Bags filled with down are less bulky than those filled with artificial fiber, but the down bags are more expensive. Look at the quilting, too — wall quilting is the warmest and the best. And check whether the zip is metal or plastic — metal ones feel like ice if you lie against them in the middle of the night!

Backpacks

The best backpacks have a lightweight metal frame with shoulder and waist straps. The frame keeps the bulk of the pack off your back. It also positions the load higher, making it easier and more comfortable to carry.

A badly organized pack will drag around your waist, so put heavy things such as your tent at the top. Breakables should go in the middle. In wet weather, line your backpack with a strong plastic bag and then put your things inside it.

Frame

Straps

Breakables

Tent

Stove

Maps

Food

Clothes

Sleeping bag

Tents

Guy line

The correct tent can make the difference between a disastrous trip and an enjoyable one, so whether you are renting or buying, choose carefully. A simple A-frame tent is fine for the occasional summer camping trip, and it is one of the cheapest. Check the weight you'll be carrying on your back as well. With their light alloy poles, many nylon tents big enough for two people weigh less than $2\frac{1}{2}$ pounds.

▲ Hammer in tent pegs at a 90° angle to the guy line. On loose soil, hammer in a crossed pair of pegs to keep them in place.

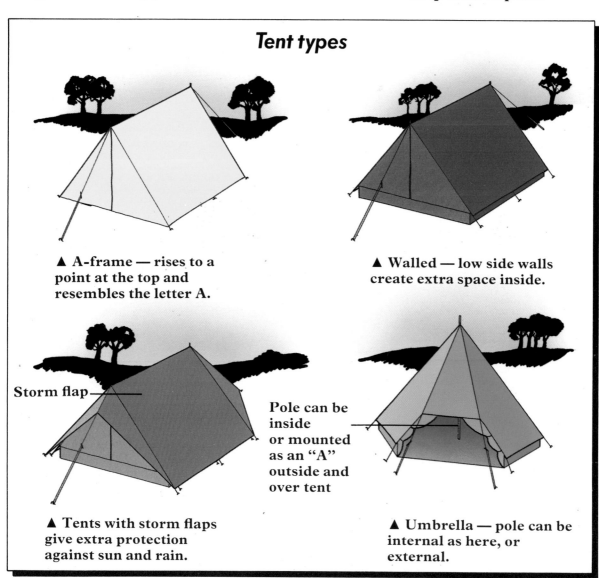

Tent types

▲ A-frame — rises to a point at the top and resembles the letter A.

▲ Walled — low side walls create extra space inside.

Storm flap

Pole can be inside or mounted as an "A" outside and over tent

▲ Tents with storm flaps give extra protection against sun and rain.

▲ Umbrella — pole can be internal as here, or external.

▲ Tents come in a wide range of types, sizes, materials, and prices. These are some of the lightweight nylon tents now available.

▼ Practice putting up your tent at home, *before* you set off on your camping trip, as managing the pegs and guy lines can be tricky at first. The storm flap goes on last and sits a little above the tent, like an outer roof. Besides keeping off the rain, it keeps the tent cool in sunny weather.

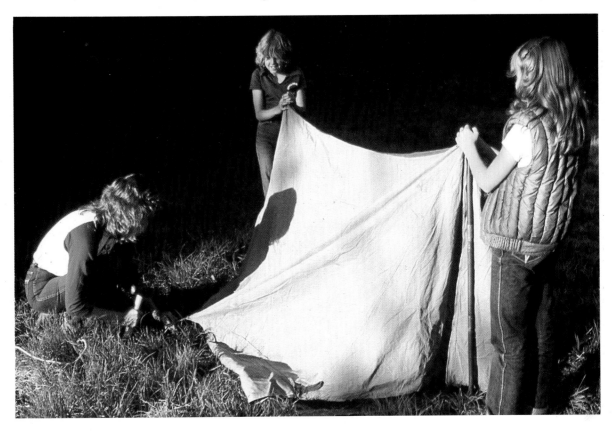

Sleeping under the stars

■ Only sleep out in the open when the weather is really warm. Nights can be cool, even when the days are very hot, so make sure you have a good sleeping bag. Check that there is some sort of shelter nearby, in case it rains and you have to scramble for cover.

Knowing how to erect a temporary shelter, or bivouac, will come in handy if you do get caught in the open when it rains. Below are two examples of a quick and easy lean-to, which you could practice erecting in your yard or (after obtaining permission) in a local park.

▶ **When sleeping in the open, use a ground cloth to stop damp seeping up into your sleeping bag.**

Bivouacs

One way of making a lean-to is to hang a ground cloth over a length of rope tied between two trees, as shown below left. Heavy stones keep the bottom edges of the lean-to in place. Below right is an even simpler version, which uses a wall or a fence for support. This is fine for calm weather, but it should not be used in windy conditions as a strong gust could drag the stones on the wall down on top of you.

Ready to go?

Route	Check that you have all of the necessary maps to cover the route you've agreed on with your friends. Contact the nearest tourism bureau for more information. List the places you'd like to visit.
Campsites	Mark these on your maps and try to book them in advance, particularly in busy seasons.
Weather	Think of things to do if the weather is bad, and places such as museums you could visit. What games do you play? Playing cards are small and light.
Supplies	Write down everything you can think of, then go through the list again and cross out all the unnecessary items. Find out what the others are taking so that you don't double up — you'll only need one camping stove between you, for instance.
Distribution	Divide the heavy or awkward items evenly — there is no need for one person to carry it all!
Emergency numbers	Give parents or guardians a copy of your route and telephone numbers for the various campsites. Write your name, home address, and telephone number on a card and keep it on you at all times.
First aid	Your basic kit should include a mild disinfectant to clean cuts and grazes, and a box of Band-Aids. Take scissors and gauze, in case you need to bandage a larger wound, and a pair of tweezers for splinters.

Disinfectant   Surgical tape   Band-Aids

Gauze   Scissors   Tweezers

Setting up camp

■ Even if you only plan to spend one night at a site, take a little time to choose the best spot for your tent. Look for dry ground which is slightly raised, so that it doesn't get boggy at the first sign of rain. Bushes and low trees will give shelter from wind and rain, but don't erect your tent under trees with branches that could snap off in a high wind.

Camping in the wild

You may not always want to stay at a reserved campground, but if you're planning to camp in the wild, be sure to obtain permission before you set up camp.

Keep well clear of fields that have livestock in them, and never erect your tent where a crop has been sown.

Check that supplies of clean, fresh water are close by before you decide on a site — hiking to get water won't be the most popular of your camping tasks!

▼ Once the camp is set up, you can use it as a base for day trips or water sports such as canoeing.

▲ If you're lucky enough to have a good view from your campsite, angle the tent opening toward it.

▲ In windy weather, be extra careful where you position the tent — and the campfire!

▲ Sleeping on a slope isn't easy or comfortable, so try to erect your tent on reasonably level ground.

▲ Pebbles soon feel like boulders when you're lying on them, so clear the base area before you put up your tent.

▲ Avoid boggy areas. If you're near the sea, don't camp on low-lying ground where a high tide might swamp you.

▲ It's convenient to be close to a store or farm where you can buy daily supplies of basic foods.

13

Around the campfire

Toasting your toes around a campfire is one of the best ways to end a day in the country, especially if someone has a harmonica or a guitar to get a singsong going. And with a little care and attention, a fire can be as safe as it is enjoyable. Make sure that you collect all the wood you need before it gets too dark to find it, and never cut fresh wood from trees or bushes.

Gas lantern

Gas stove

▶ It isn't always practical to have a campfire, particularly if dry wood is in short supply. A quick and simple alternative is a small camping stove with a disposable gas cylinder.

The latest ones have a built-in sparking system, which lights the gas as soon as you turn it on. Camping-gas lanterns are a good idea for general illumination at night.

Making a campfire

Ask the landowner's permission before collecting wood and lighting a fire and, for your own and others' safety, always follow these simple rules:

☑ Build the fire downwind of your tent, at least 6 to 10 feet away from it.
☑ The fire shouldn't be near bushes or under low trees.
☑ Clear the area of anything else that might catch fire, especially dry leaves and twigs — the campfire is the only blaze you want going.
☑ Follow the steps below and on the right to learn how to make a fire without damaging a grassy area or scarring the landscape.

▲ Cut into a 3-foot square area of grass. Divide the square into four quarters.

▲ Roll back the turf and store it upside down in a cool place, ready to be replaced later.

▲ If the fireplace is wet, line it with stones or sand. Make a stone border around the edges.

▲ Nothing tastes quite as delicious as a meal cooked over a campfire!

Extinguish the fire with water when you've finished with it. When the embers are thoroughly cold and wet, scatter them somewhere out of sight and return the stones to where you found them. If you then replace the squares of turf, treading them lightly back into place, there should be little sign left of your fire.

▲ Push a stick into the fireplace, then build a nest of crumpled paper and small sticks.

▲ Light the paper first. When the sticks catch fire, slowly add bigger chunks of dry wood.

▲ Keep adding wood until there is a good blaze going. Watch over the fire at all times.

Outdoor kitchen

■ Rule one for the camp cook is "keep it simple." Preparing fussy food isn't easy in a well-equipped kitchen, let alone at a campsite. Rule two is "keep it clean" — don't get grass or dirt in the food. Rule three is "cut down on the pots and pans." As well as being tasty, one-pot meals such as stews will leave your assistants with less dish washing to complain about!

▼ The campfire kitchen should include the basic utensils shown below. Make sure you take tough equipment that will survive the rigors of camping — items made of metal or plastic are best as these will not break if they get dropped. The can opener should be a multipurpose type which will also open bottles.

▶ Camping-gas stoves can be used for any cooking which involves boiling or frying. You will get more heat from a stove if you erect a windscreen for it, as even a light breeze will blow heat away. Make sure you prop the windscreen securely to stop it falling over. The one shown here is especially made for the job.

Teakettle

1–2 saucepans

Frying pan

Plates and bowls

Cups

Can opener

Knives

Forks

Spoons

Bread knife

Spatula

Soup spoon

Eco-sense

☑ Bury vegetable peelings and food waste that will rot in the ground.

☑ Put your other trash in a strong plastic bag, ready to be emptied into a garbage can or taken with you when you leave.

☑ Be sure to bag up all cans and bottles. Animals or campers could cut themselves on sharp edges, while bright sun focussing through glass could start a fire.

☑ Suspend the trash bag well above ground level to stop animals tearing it open and scattering the contents.

☑ Wash the dishes as soon as the meal is over — insects and creepy-crawlies love dirty pots!

Food planning

There's nothing like fresh air for working up an appetite, so make sure you plan a big breakfast and an evening meal each day. It's best to take a picnic if you're spending the day away from camp, with chocolate and protein bars to eat as energy snacks mid-morning and afternoon. Don't forget something to drink!

Planning a day's food isn't difficult, and it's a job you can all take turns doing. Here is a food plan for a weekend trip, to give you a few ideas.

BREAKFAST

Day one

Fruit
Cereal
Fried egg and bacon
Biscuits

Day two

Fruit juice
Cereal
Scrambled eggs on bread, with sausages

LUNCH

Ham or cheese sandwiches
Pickle
Slice of carrot cake
Yogurt or fruit

Cheese, tomato, or peanut butter and jelly sandwiches
Nuts and Rasins
Yogurt or fruit

EVENING MEAL

Packet or can of soup
Hot dog
Buns
Salad
Lemon cake

Grapefruit
Vegetable stew, or meat and vegetable stew
Potatoes wrapped in tinfoil and baked in the camp-fire embers
Canned peaches

Tying knots

On a camping trip it's a good idea to take along some thin rope or string — and useful if you know beforehand how to tie knots with it. There are dozens of different knots you can learn, but you should find that the four shown here will suit most requirements. Although they may appear complicated, with a little practice you'll find them easy to master and remember.

Clove hitch

This knot is used to make non-slip attachments to posts and other solid objects. Fixing a rope between two trees is just one of the ways a clove hitch will come in handy around the campsite.
1. Make two loops.
2. Place one loop on top of the other.
3. Carefully slip the pair of loops over the top of the post.
4. Pull both ends of the rope to make the knot grip tightly.

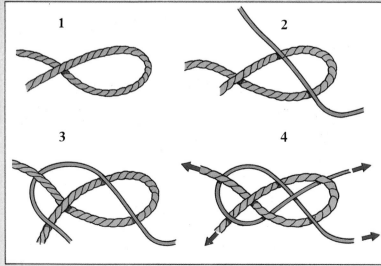

Carrick bend

Use this knot to join two ropes. It grips well, but it is also easy to untie.
1. Loop the end of one rope.
2. Lay the second rope over the first.
3. Take the second rope under and between the crossed first rope.
4. Weave the second rope under and through the first loop. Pull the ends of both ropes tightly to finish the knot.

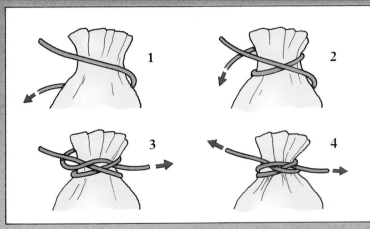

Sack knot

This knot is ideal for keeping animals out of trash bags.

1. Loop the neck of the bag.
2. Take one end around to make another loop.
3. Take the end of the second loop over, then under itself.
4. Pull both rope ends to close the bag tightly.

Rope sling

A sling is a very useful way of carrying a container which doesn't have a handle.

1. Center the container on the rope.
2. Tie the rope ends once across the top.
3. Open one loop, pulling it sideways to make a noose under the lip of the container.
4. Tighten the noose and lift the container.

▼ One way of using a sling knot – to carry water.

Map reading

■ Once you've set up camp, it's time to go exploring. Your best friend now is your map. Use it to plan your route for the day, and remember to take it with you! The time to practice your map-reading skills is *before* you set off though, not when you're out in the woods on a dark and stormy night, not sure where you are...

▼ Plan your day's walk carefully and don't try to go too far — an average pace is 2—2½ miles an hour. Check your map often, to keep on the right track.

A useful map scale is 1:25,000, which means 4 inches of map covers 1 mile of land. All natural features are shown, as well as towns, villages, and some buildings.

To use a map to find out where you are, begin by looking around you and identifying big features such as hills, forests, and towns. When you've found these on the map, look for a smaller feature closer to you, such as a road or bridge. Now line up the map so the features around you match the symbols on it.

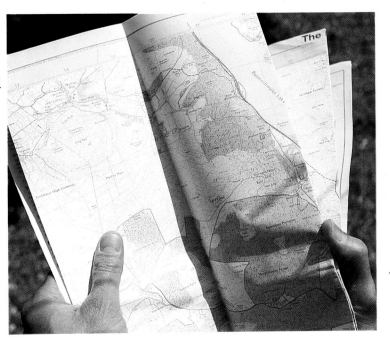

► The geographical outlines or contours of the land are given on large-scale maps. Contour lines such as those on the right show height above sea level, and measurements are usually given on the lines themselves.

Look at the contour lines when you are planning your hike, as they show whether land is hilly or flat. The going is steep when the spaces between the contour lines are narrow, while widely spaced contours indicate gentle slopes. And as you can see on the right, you can also identify particular landforms from their contour patterns.

Hill

Valley

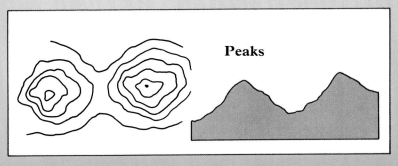

Peaks

Sun and star navigation

■ Navigation is the art of finding your way, and it's helped by a good sense of direction and a compass. Below and opposite are some tips on how to navigate without a map or a compass, in case you ever get completely lost. If you choose one direction and stick to it, eventually you'll find a road or a house where you can ask for help. Only head off if you can see where you're going, though. If it is foggy or the night is dark, stay where you are and keep warm until help arrives or the weather improves.

▶ **If you find yourself lost without a compass, you can find your way using the Sun. To do this you need a watch face with hands (for digital watches see below right).**

In the northern hemisphere, point the hour hand at the Sun. South is halfway between the hour hand and 12 o'clock.

Northern hemisphere

Sun

Point hour hand toward the Sun

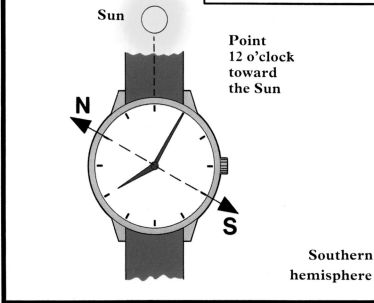

Sun

Point 12 o'clock toward the Sun

Southern hemisphere

◀ **To use your watch-compass in the southern hemisphere, point 12 o'clock toward the Sun. The north–south line runs halfway between the hour hand and 12 o'clock.**

If you don't have a watch with hands, simply draw a watch face on a piece of paper, with the hands showing the correct time.

Finding north

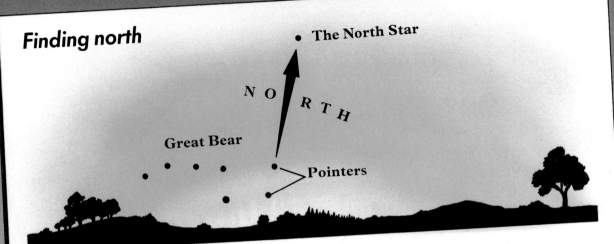

The North Star

NORTH

Great Bear

Pointers

If you ever lose your way at night you can use the stars as a guide, just as ships' navigators have done for centuries. If you are in the northern hemisphere, begin by finding the constellation called Ursa Major, the Great Bear. The pair of stars on the right of the base are called the Pointers, because a straight line through them points to the North Star, also known as the polestar. If you turn to face the North Star you are looking north, with west on your left, east on your right, and south behind you.

Finding south

Southern Cross

Four times the length of the Cross

Imaginary point in the sky

SOUTH

If you are in the southern hemisphere, you need to find Crux, the Southern Cross. It's quite a small constellation, so look along the faint band of the Milky Way until you come to the dark patch called the Coal Sack. This marks the edge of the Southern Cross stars. Make the cross by imagining lines between the two closest stars and the two farthest apart. Now extend one line as shown above, making it four times as deep as the cross. If you face the point at the end of this imaginary line, you are looking due south.

Into the unknown

■ Armed with your map-reading and navigation skills, you're now ready to face the unknown and enjoy it. Even so, telling someone at the campsite your planned route and when you expect to return is a wise precaution in case you get lost or are injured in some way.

You might like to take a notebook and a small camera or sketchpad with you, to record your journey and any interesting wildlife you may discover.

▶ A small frameless knapsack is ideal for carrying things you'll need during the day. Spare clothes will depend on the weather, but don't forget a rainproof jacket.

Take a flashlight and a whistle to signal for help in an emergency — repeat the SOS signal of three short, three long, three short whistle blasts (or flashlight flashes at night).

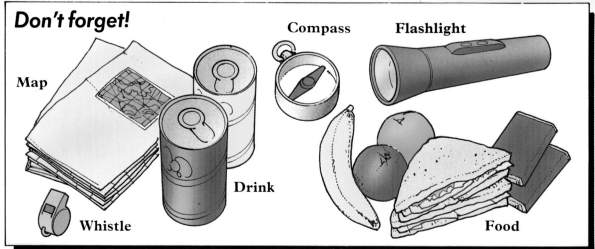

Don't forget!

Map

Whistle

Drink

Compass

Flashlight

Food

▲ Exploring the wilderness can be fascinating, but keep an eye on your watch and allow time to get back to camp before nightfall.

The Country Code

Here are some reminders to treat the country with the respect it deserves — enjoy the scenery, but leave it as you found it.

☑ Close gates after you, even if you find them left open.

☑ Don't pick or damage wild flowers or plants.

☑ Be wary of snakes, especially rattlesnakes and copperheads. It is a good idea to carry a snakebit kit.

☑ Keep to paths across farmland, and walk around fields if a path isn't clear — even grass is a valuable crop!

☑ Take your trash back to the camp with you, together with any other litter you come across.

☑ Avoid noise pollution too — leave radios at home or keep the sound down.

Weather watching

■ The weather is always changing, so checking the daily weather forecast can mean the difference between being safe and being sorry.

Most changes in weather take place along fronts. These are the areas, or zones, where a cold air mass meets a warm air mass. The three main types of front are illustrated below — you'll find that learning the front symbols will make the weather maps seen in newspapers and on television a little easier to understand.

Warm front

In a warm front, an advancing mass of warm air slides up and over a retreating mass of cold air. Although warm fronts often produce light rain or snow, clearer skies and a rise in temperature follow their passing.

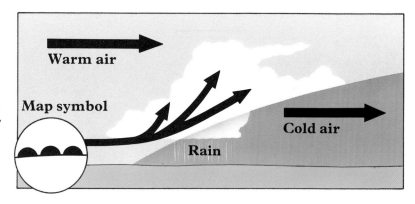

Cold front

This is when an advancing mass of cold air moves under a mass of warm air, forcing it upward. Cold fronts cause sudden changes in the weather, often producing short, heavy showers. Colder weather follows their passing.

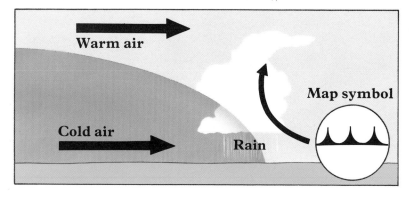

Occluded front

When cold fronts catch up with warm ones, they lift up the warmer air above the Earth's surface. These occluded fronts bring a mixture of cold and warm front weather conditions — heavy, low clouds, and long periods of rain or snow.

Cloud types

However hard forecasters work at finding out about the weather, there are no guarantees that their predictions will be correct. When you're out in the wilderness, recognizing the signs in the sky is just as important a survival technique as being able to read the symbols on a map.

1. **Stratus** — low thick sheets of fog-like cloud, often producing light rain.

2. **Nimbostratus** — shapeless dark-gray cloud, shedding rain in summer and snow in winter.

3. **Stratocumulus** — rolls of light and dark cloud.

4. **Cumulus** — fluffy white cloud seen in fair weather.

5. **Cumulonimbus** — towering mass of dark cloud, giving rain, hail, and thunderstorms.

6. **Altostratus** — sheets of pale, gray cloud, which can thicken to bring rain.

7. **Altocumulus** — gray streaks and patches of cloud, usually seen in fine settled weather.

8. **Cirrostratus** — high thin haze, which can mean rain or snow is coming.

9. **Cirrocumulus** — small fleecy balls of high cloud, like ripples, often seen before rain or storms.

10. **Cirrus** — thin high cloud often seen when the weather is fine. If curled in "hooks," rain on the way.

Weather-wise camping

■ Cold, wind, fog, and electrical storms are enemies of campers and hikers. In the event of an electrical storm you can avoid being struck by following certain safety measures during thunderstorms: stay away from water and metal objects. If you are in an open area, sit or crouch down. If you are stranded in a forest, take cover beneath low trees. Always keep an eye on the weather.

▶ **A lightweight "space blanket," made of shiny foil, is useful for cold weather emergencies.**

In mild, damp weather rubber boots lined with a "breathing" material can be useful.

Defense against wind and rain

Camping in bad weather needs special action. In really high winds, lay heavy rocks over all the tent pegs, after treading the pegs as far into the ground as possible. If camping on a slope in wet weather, dig a shallow ditch on the uphill side above the tent to stop water flooding in.

Heavy rock

Drainage ditch

Danger – fog!

Lay stones behind you, one every few feet.

In foggy weather, it's easy to lose your sense of direction and walk in circles. This can be very dangerous in boggy or mountainous country, so stay where you are and keep warm until help arrives or the weather improves. In fairly open country, with even ground, you can hold a course through fog by laying a straight-line trail of stones behind you.

▲ There are lots of folklore sayings which claim to predict the weather. Some of these are quite reliable, such as "red sky at night, shepherd's delight." The Sun can only be seen low on the western horizon, reddening the sky, if there is little or no advancing cold front cloud to block our view. That's why fine days usually follow a red evening sky.

Other weather sayings are based on observations of animal behavior. "Spiders' webs bigger, weather's going to be better" seems to be true more often than not.

You might like to make a collection of weather sayings, and then test them on your camping trip.

Fighting the cold

■ The human body needs to maintain an inside temperature of around 98.6°F. People can become very ill if this goes up or down by just a few degrees. That is why keeping warm is your most important survival tactic when the temperature drops. If you plan a camping trip in a country with a very cold climate, the correct protective clothing and equipment are essential.

► Canadian winter camping. Inside the tent, sheltered from the bitter winds, campers stay snug and warm. In this time-lapse photograph, stars seem to wheel as streaks of light around the single point of the North Star.

The wind-chill factor

Moving air cools bare flesh a lot more quickly than still air — that's why people enjoy a breeze on a hot summer day. Wind is not so pleasant in winter or at night, though. And as the temperature drops and the wind speed increases, windchill can become a real menace. Cooled by the wind, flesh temperature can drop below that of the still air, making frostbite a danger. In really cold climates, windchill can be a killer.

To prevent loss of body heat, clothing should be wind and waterproof. Wear lots of layers, because the air trapped between the clothes acts as an insulator, keeping you warm. Fabrics such as wool are best, as they let the skin breathe.

Air temperature °F		50°F	32°F	14°F	
Wind speed in mph	5	48	28	10	Windchill temperatures
	10	41	17	− 4	
	20	32	5	− 20	
	40	27	− 6	− 33	

Out in the midday Sun

■ When the weather is hot, one of the ways the body keeps its temperature down is by sweating — the liquid which is evaporated from the skin takes heat with it. If you're planning to walk in the heat, drinking enough to replace the water your body loses by sweating is vital.

Keeping cool so that you don't sweat so much is also important, as is protection against sunburn. Light colored clothes are best, as they reflect the Sun's rays. Wear a hat, and use a sunscreening lotion not a suntan lotion. Rest in the shade in the middle of the day, when the sun is hottest.

▼ **The hottest part of the day is when the Sun is high overhead. Here, camel trekkers break at noon for a rest in the shade of some trees. In hot countries, camels make ideal pack animals as they can survive for long periods using the water stored in their humps.**

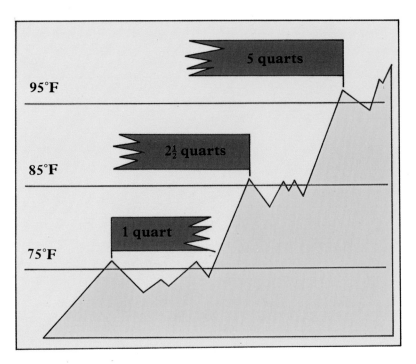

5 quarts

95°F

2½ quarts

85°F

1 quart

75°F

◄ This chart shows the minimum amount of water needed by our bodies each day. The hotter it gets, and the more exercise we do, the more water we need as our bodies lose heat by sweating. Although humans can survive many days without food, they can last only a short while without water.

Protection from the Sun

Clothes are your first line of defense, both in reducing water loss through sweating and in protecting against sunburn. Your head and neck must be covered. If you don't have a hat, use a cloth or spare shirt — and if you've plenty of water, dampening the material will make you cooler.

◄ The French képi protects the back of the neck from the sun. Make your own képi, using a clean white handkerchief, kept in place by a lightweight cap.

▲ If you have no sunglasses, you can make eyeshades out of a piece of cardboard, tied at the ends with elastic or string. Cut a pair of eye slits with a knife. Trim off any loose bits of cardboard before you wear the shades.

A test of map-reading and navigation

■ Orienteering, a form of cross-country racing, is an exciting and competitive hiking sport which will help you to develop your map-reading skills further, while enjoying time outside. For a typical event, an area is specially mapped and checkpoints are set up within it. Competitors use their map and compass to navigate the quickest way between the various checkpoints.

▼ **The Silva compass was specially developed in Sweden for the sport of orienteering.**

▶ **Suitable clothes for orienteering include a lightweight tracksuit to protect limbs from scratches. There's no need for heavy clothing — running will keep you warm. Add a pair of comfortable tennis shoes, or special shoes with studs to increase grip on muddy tracks. Take a whistle to summon help in an emergency.**

Carrying cord

Compass needle

Magnifying glass

Sides marked in millimeters and inches

Transparent plastic body can be seen through when laid on map

▲ ▶ **Checkpoints are shown on orienteering maps by numbered circles. On the course, they are identified by red and white buckets or nylon markers.**

To prove that they've visited all the checkpoints and haven't cheated, all competitors carry a special card. Each time they reach a checkpoint they use a pin punch to clip a particular area of the card.

Needle punch tied to post

Each checkpoint has a different punch pattern

Fastest across the map

■ Competitors in orienteering events run different routes, depending on their age and skills. So don't follow other people if you get confused — they could be on a different course! Orientate yourself on your map, and if necessary return to a familiar feature and try again.

As well as keeping track of your position on the map, it's important to think of good routes to the next checkpoint. If there's a hill in the way, is it quicker to walk a shorter distance over the top or to run a longer distance around it?

▶ Having studied your map, you need to head for the next checkpoint as quickly as possible. As your "map memory" improves, you will require fewer stops to check where you are going.

Orienteering events

There are various types of orienteering competition, although the idea behind them remains the same — navigating on the move across unknown country.

Cross-country
This is the most common type of event. Competitors race across a set course, checking in at checkpoints.

Score events
Lots of checkpoints are set up. Each of these has a different score value, and the highest scoring ones are usually farthest from the start line. The winning competitor is the person who collects the highest score within a set time, often one hour.

Relay race
The usual entry is a team of three, each running one third of the course. Unlike most orienteering events, there is a mass start, and the winner is the first to cross the finishing line.

Night orienteering
For nighttime events, courses are planned to allow for the fact that competitors will be using flashlights to find their way. Not a good idea for beginners, but great fun once you are used to daytime competitions.

Line courses
These are usually training events. Competitors are given the line of the course, but not the position of the checkpoints. Following the line will lead you to the checkpoints. If you wander off course, you'll miss them and lose points.

Map memory
This is another training event. The course has to be memorized, one section at a time. Taking part in these events builds up confidence and speed.

Ski orienteering
An event for countries where cross-country skiing is made possible by good snow cover in winter. The rules are much the same as for normal orienteering, but the courses are longer because skis are faster than feet!

▶ This is not quite the rough-country orienteering it looks — in fact, the race is taking place in a wooded city park. But such urban courses give beginners a good introduction to the sport and prepare competitors for the problems involved in navigating out in the woods. Out in the country, the terrain may be sandy, hilly, wooded slopes, or rocky forests. Each course has its own set of problems.

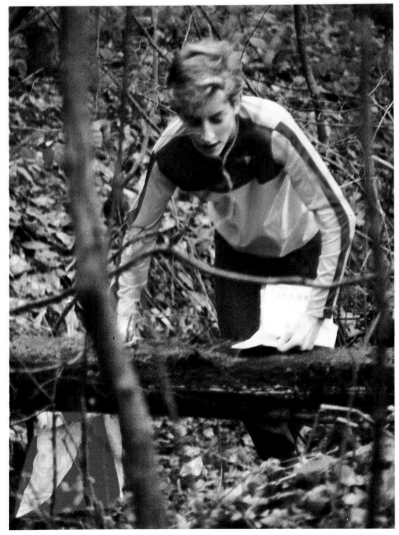

Taking pictures

Combining photographs with a diary will make a record of your camping trip much more colorful. Here's some information about the type of photographic equipment that will stand up to the hiking trail.

▼ These deer were photographed in Yosemite National Park, California. A compact camera is ideal for getting good results from unexpected sights like this.

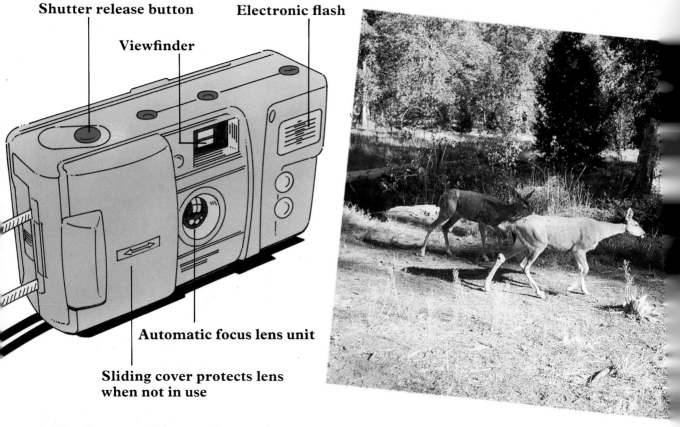

Shutter release button

Electronic flash

Viewfinder

Automatic focus lens unit

Sliding cover protects lens when not in use

▲ The "compact" is one of the most useful types of cameras. This one has automatic focus, light exposure, and film advance, so it's quick and easy to use. And because it's small and light, it can be carried in a pocket, loaded and ready for action. It also has a built-in electronic flash for low-light and night shots.

Many compact cameras have a sliding cover to protect the lens. Opening the cover switches on the camera.

The more recent models are powered by lithium batteries which have a five-year life. If your camera takes ordinary batteries, make sure you carry a spare set — batteries always seem to

fail at awkward moments.

If you plan on doing water sports such as canoeing, it's worth taking a waterproof camera. These can generally survive a brief dip, and some even float if you drop them overboard. "Splashproof" cameras can survive rain, but they don't like going for a swim.

Glossary

Breathing materials
General name for those clothing fabrics which keep you warm, while letting the natural moisture from your body out. This allows your skin to "breathe," so you don't get sweaty. A natural breathing fabric is wool.

Checkpoint
One of the stops on an orienteering course. At each checkpoint, competitors use a punch marked with a different pin pattern to record that they have been to the point.

Compact camera
General name for pocket-sized automatic cameras.

Frame backpack
Knapsack mounted on a sturdy but lightweight metal frame, to which the shoulder and waist harness are attached. Using a frame, the knapsack is kept slightly off the back, which means any lumps in your packload don't dig painful holes in your body. Also, the load stays high up, not slipping to waist level. High-mounted loads are easier to carry.
    A frameless backpack is only suitable for light loads.

Ground cloth
Waterproof sheet laid down between a camper and the ground. Its purpose is to stop dampness rising from the soil.

Guy lines
Ropes which keep a tent up.

Képi
Flat cap, with fabric flap at the back to protect the neck from hot sun. Képis were first used by soldiers in the French Foreign Legion, based in the African Sahara desert.

Lean-to
A temporary camp in the open. A lean-to can be made from waterproof sheets slung over convenient trees, bushes, or low walls.

Map scales
Maps come in various scales according to their use. A popular size for walkers is 1:25,000, or 4 inches to 1 mile. Orienteering maps are often scaled to 1:15,000 which allows much more detail to be shown.

Mountain bike
Off-road bicycle equipped with sturdy frame, thick tires, and low gears.

SOS
Emergency "help" signal, consisting of . . . – – – . . . This dot-dash-dot signal can be made by radio, puffed with smoke, flashed with a flashlight, or even banged on a tin lid. The letters SOS stand for "Save Our Souls."

Space blanket
Thin plastic sheet, covered with a reflective metallic coating. Useful in emergencies as it keeps off wind and retains body heat. Weighs less than $3\frac{1}{2}$ ounces so can be carried in a pocket.

Standing camp
Campsite used for several days (or even a complete vacation) as a base from which to go out exploring.

Sunscreen
A cream which can be smoothed onto the skin to prevent burning by the ultraviolet light in sunshine. Small amounts of ultraviolet light cause a healthy suntan — too much causes bad skin burns.

Windchill factor
Amount by which wind cools a body even more than the temperature of the air. The more wind, the colder you get.

Index